GOOD NEWS FOR

Moms

WORDS OF WISDOM
AND INSPIRATION FOR MOMS

COMPILED BY LISA KING

CROSSWAY BOOKS · WHEATON, ILLINOIS
A DIVISION OF GOOD NEWS PUBLISHERS

Good News for Moms

Copyright © 1998 by Good News Publishers

Published by
CROSSWAY BOOKS
A division of Good News Publishers
1300 Crescent Street, Wheaton, Illinois 60187

All rights reserved. No part of this publication may be reproduced, stored in a retrieval system or transmitted in any form by any means, electronic, mechanical, photocopy, recording or otherwise, without the prior permission of the publisher, except as provided by USA copyright law.

Scripture taken from the HOLY BIBLE: NEW INTERNATIONAL VERSION ®. Copyright © 1973, 1978, 1984 by International Bible Society. Used by permission of Zondervan Publishing House. All rights reserved.

The "NIV" and "New International Version" trademarks are registered in the United States Patent and Trademark Office by International Bible Society. Use of either trademark requires the permission of International Bible Society.

First printing, 1998. Cover and book design: Cindy Kiple. Printed in the United States of America

LIBRARY OF CONGRESS CATALOGING-IN-PUBLICATION DATA
Good news for moms : words of wisdom and inspiration for moms / compiled by Lisa King.
    p.   cm.
    1. Mothers—Religious life—Quotations, maxims, etc.
2. Motherhood—Religious aspects—Christianity—Quotations, maxims, etc.   I. King, Lisa.
    BV4847.G66 1998   242'.6431—dc21   98-10299
                    ISBN 0-89107-996-3

06   05   04   03   02   01   00   99   98
15   14   13   12   11   10   9   8   7   6   5   4   3   2   1

Especially for You

It is our desire that *Good News for Moms* encourage, inspire, and challenge you in your God-given role as a mother. He has entrusted you with a great and noble responsibility. We want to support you in that task.

Through the promises of Scripture and the insights of godly men and women from the past and present, we trust that this little book will enable you to better fulfill God's call as a mom. Our prayer is that some kernel of truth or piece of wisdom you find in these pages will lift your spirit, warm your heart, or challenge your mind. And in doing so that God will work through you to touch those who mean the most to you.

If our calling is to be mothers,
let's be mothers with all our hearts—
gladly, simply, and humbly.

ELISABETH ELLIOT

Sons are a heritage from the Lord,

children a reward from him.

PSALM 127:3

*G*od has placed the lives of your children in

your hands. They will bear the imprint

of your love and concern

throughout their lives.

LOUISE SHATTUCK

From the moment of conception,

having a child is a partnership

with heaven.

RON HUTCHCRAFT
5 Needs Your Child Must Have Met at Home

Children are a lot like chickens . . .

they need room to squawk,

lay a few eggs,

flap their wings,

even to fly the coop.

CHARLES SWINDOLL
The Strong Family

By wisdom a house is built, and through understanding it is established; through knowledge its rooms are filled with rare and beautiful treasures.

PROVERBS 24:3-4

When a parent makes a promise—and
determines to stick by it—a child's
trust and confidence build.
Confidence not only in
the adult, but in God.

JONI EARECKSON TADA
Tell Me the Promises

$\mathcal{I}$ long to accomplish a great and noble task, but it is my chief duty to accomplish humble tasks as though they were great and noble. The world is moved along, not only by the mighty shoves of its heroes, but also by the aggregate of the tiny pushes of each honest worker. ❧

HELEN KELLER
The Treasure Chest

Lovely, complicated wrappings

Sheath the gift of one-day-more;

Breathless, I untie the package—

Never lived this day before!

GLORIA GAITHER

Nothing in this life can bring a
greater sense of joy and fulfillment
than your family.

KURT BRUNER
Parents Resource Bible

Children's children are a crown to
the aged, and parents are the
pride of their children.

PROVERBS 17:6

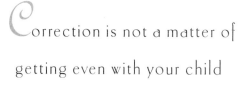

Correction is not a matter of

getting even with your child

ADRIAN ROGERS
Ten Secrets for a Successful Family

It's not what your child thinks of you now that's as important as what he thinks of you twenty years from now.

SUSAN YATES

*I*f we fail to recognize that mothering is an art that has a profound impact on our entire society, we are in danger of losing something very precious indeed. ❧

DEBRA EVANS
Christian Woman's Guide to Sexuality

The way your children turn out

does not depend on what you do,

but rather what you are.

LUANNE SHACKLEFORD
A Survivor's Guide to Home Schooling

Now may the Lord of peace himself
give you peace at all times and
in every way. The Lord
be with all of you.

2 THESSALONIANS 3:16

Motherhood is teaching me that
everyone in this harsh world needs
tenderness and a kind word.

ANNETTE LAPLACA

$\mathcal{C}$hildren may be the little trumpet players who

bring us to our senses, and to our knees.

BILLY GRAHAM
The Faithful Christian

☙

A parent would do better to sow weeds in a field from which he expects to derive food for his family than by his own bad behavior to nurture evil in the heart of his child.

CHARLES HODGE

I tell you the truth, unless you change and become like little children, you will never enter the kingdom of heaven. Therefore, whoever humbles himself like this child is the greatest in the kingdom of heaven.

JESUS, MATTHEW 18:3-4

I heard the voice of Jesus say:
"Come unto Me and rest;
Lay down, thou weary one, lay down
Thy head upon My breast!"
I came to Jesus as I was,
Weary, and worn, and sad;
I found in Him a resting place,
And He has made me glad.

HORATIUS BONAR

I can't do a lot, but I do not want
to be guilty of doing nothing.

SUSAN HUNT
By Design

There can never be an excess of
honor within the family.

ROLF ZETTERSTEN
Parents Resource Bible

*D*o not think that just because you have conceived, carried, and finally given birth to your little one, you automatically know your child. Knowing him or her takes time, careful observation, diligent study, prayer, concentration, help from above, and, yes, wisdom. ❧

CHARLES SWINDOLL
The Strong Family

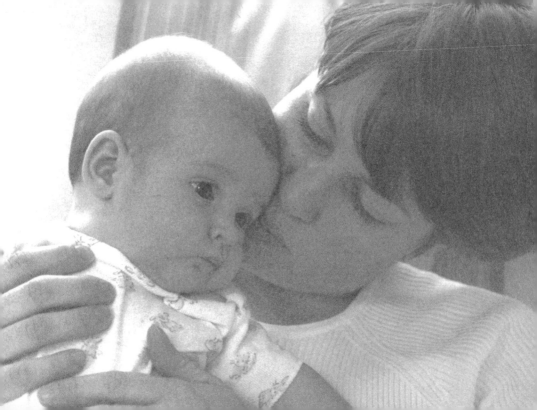

Know therefore that the Lord
your God is God; he is the faithful
God, keeping his covenant of love
to a thousand generations of
those who love him and
keep his commands.

DEUTERONOMY 7:9

The greatest influence on earth,
whether for good or evil,
is possessed by women.

JOHN ANGELL JAMES

The true character of a person is seen not in

momentary heroics but in the thump-packed

humdrum of day-to-day living.

MAX LUCADO

Let your life be a message that
your children will never forget.

HARRY VAN'T KERKHOFF

❧

$\mathcal{I}$f the love of God for the human race is as

great as the love of parents for their children,

then it is truly great and ardent. ❧

MARTIN LUTHER
The Best from All His Works

Why if you have told your children never to interrupt you, do they interrupt you with little whispers as if whispering were better?

WALTER WANGERIN, JR.
Little Lamb Who Made Thee?

God demonstrates
his own love for us in this:
While we were still sinners,
Christ died for us.

ROMANS 5:8

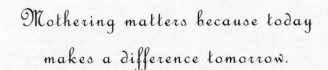

*Mothering matters because today
makes a difference tomorrow.*

ELISA MORGAN
What Every Mom Needs

hrough many dangers, toils and snares

I have already come;

'Tis grace that brought me safe thus far,

And grace will lead me home.

JOHN NEWTON

A mother is a walking encyclopedia. Her children expect her to know where the sun goes at night, how jet propulsion works, what the principal exports of Thailand are, and where kittens come from.

LOUISE SHATTUCK

Home is like the eye of the storm:
through any chaos, heartbreak, or
loss it is a place where one
sees clearly that running
away is not the answer.

MARLEE ALEX

Love and discipline go hand in hand, and I thank God for giving me a father and mother who taught me it was so.

JANETTE OKE

$\mathcal{G}$ood parenting has a way of crossing
generations to inspire its children's children.

CALVIN MILLER

I am the way and the truth

and the life.

No one comes to the Father

except through me.

JESUS, JOHN 14:6

To be genuinely concerned about the interests of others, you must be genuinely committed to the interests of Christ. ✍

JOSEPH STOWELL

Whatever God gives you to do, do it as well as you can. This is the best possible preparation for what He may want you to do next.

GEORGE MACDONALD

God gave children parents
because they need us.

LUANNE SHACKLEFORD
A Survivor's Guide to Home Schooling

Above all, love each other deeply,

because love covers over a

multitude of sins.

1 PETER 4:8

I suppose our kids did as much wrong as anyone else's. But I think they turned out better than some, because no matter what they did wrong, I never shut down on them emotionally. Every time they entered a room where I was, I was delighted, and they could see it.

UNKNOWN

Forgiveness is the starting point
for resolving life's most
troubling problems.

JOHN MACARTHUR
The Freedom and Power of Forgiveness

If any of you lacks wisdom, he should ask God, who gives generously to all without finding fault, and it will be given to him.

JAMES 1:5

Truth and excellence have a way of springing up all over the world, and our role as parents is to teach our children how to find and enjoy the riches of God and to reject what is mediocre and unworthy of Him.

GLADYS HUNT
Christian Mom's Idea Book

Help us, O Lord, when we want
to do the right thing, but know not what
it is. But help us most when we know
perfectly well what we ought to do,
and do not want to do it.

PETER MARSHALL
The Treasure Chest

Tell it to your children, and let your children tell it to their children, and their children to the next generation.

JOEL 1:3

Your child needs to know that he
or she is special—and that no
one's opinion matters as much
as yours and God's.

RON HUTCHCRAFT

$\mathcal{L}$istening—not very expensive, but it's

probably the most valuable gift

we'll ever give our children.

ELAINE MINAMIDE

We have only this moment,

sparkling like a star in our hand . . .

and melting like a snowflake.

Let us use it before it is too late.

MARIE BEYNON RAY

The magnificence of His handiwork is seen in the tumbling seas, in a sunset slashing the Grand Canyon. How much of this beauty we bring into our homes and our lives is limited only by our appreciation and desire for it. ❧

CATHERINE MARSHALL
Something More

Our children give us permission to play.

SUSAN CARD

Love is patient, love is kind. It does not envy, it does not boast, it is not proud. It is not rude, it is not self-seeking, it is not easily angered, it keeps no record of wrongs. Love does not delight in evil but rejoices with the truth. It always protects, always trusts, always hopes, always perseveres.

1 CORINTHIANS 13:4-7

Often your child doesn't want toys.
She wants you, made by God,
batteries not included.

LAURIE WINSLOW SARGENT

The raising of children can seem an eternity when you are in the midst of it, but when it is over it seems but a season.

R. KENT HUGHES

A good man generally comes
of a good mother.

C. H. SPURGEON

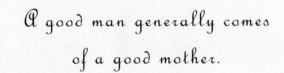

Fortunately, we are permitted to make a few mistakes with our children. No one can expect to do everything right, and it is not the few errors that destroy a child.

JAMES DOBSON

All your sons will be taught by
the Lord, and great will be
your children's peace.

ISAIAH 54:13

Children who are led into friendship with

God live with a quiet assurance

of his protection.

JUDITH MONROE

❧

I can't choose my child's temperament, but I can influence its outcome.

MARTHA SEARS

Even a child is known
by his actions, by whether his
conduct is pure and right.

PROVERBS 20:11

If you fail to tell your children the truth, your home is on the road to disaster.

ADRIAN ROGERS

Ten Secrets for a Successful Family

God doesn't delight in work that grows solely out of duty. If I receive His crown of glory, it won't be because I have chosen to stay home with my kids, but because I willingly and eagerly served Him as a parent to the boys that He has entrusted to me.

MARIAN LIAUTAUD

Mom and Dad were wise enough to broaden my knowledge of God beyond going to Sunday school, saying grace at dinner, and memorizing a lot of Bible verses. They understood that every dimension of our lives is indeed spiritual.

JONI EARECKSON TADA

It is important to have training
and discipline in the home—and not
just for the family dog!

BILLY GRAHAM

Charm is deceptive, and beauty is fleeting; but a woman who fears the Lord is to be praised.

PROVERBS 31:30

May I run the race before me
Strong and brave to face the foe,
Looking only unto Jesus
As I onward go.

KATE WILKINSON

Train your child in the way in which you know you should have gone yourself.

C. H. SPURGEON

There is nothing sweeter than the

heart of a pious mother.

MARTIN LUTHER

*G*ood parents don't waste time warning

their children what they shouldn't do

because they're too busy modeling

what they should do.

JANIS LONG HARRIS
What Good Parents Have in Common

As a mother comforts her child,

so will I comfort you....

ISAIAH 66:13A

Our kids are like two-legged mirrors, reflecting a lot of what is inside us. Sometimes the reflection is amusing, sometimes it's affirming, other times it's alarming. When parents look at their children, they ultimately find they are also looking at themselves.

RON HUTCHCRAFT
5 Needs Your Child Must Have Met at Home

The poor teacher stands where he
is and beckons the pupil come to him.
The good teacher goes to where the
pupil is, takes him, and leads
him to where he ought to go.

AQUINAS

We all want to be "normal," but what is normal? Normal is a setting on the dryer—it has nothing to do with people! Besides, normal is not our goal—Christlikeness is.

PATSY CLAIRMONT

How far you go in life depends on your being tender with the young, compassionate with the aged, sympathetic with the striving, and tolerant of the weak and of the strong. Because someday in your life you will have been all of these. ❧

GEORGE WASHINGTON CARVER
The Strong Family

To grow the best memories, our kids have to know that sometimes we seek out their company not because we know we should, but because we just can't resist. They need to know we're not merely committed to them but crazy about them.

KAREN SCALF LINAMEN

How great is the love the Father
has lavished on us, that we should
be called the children of God!
And that is what we are.

1 JOHN 3:1A

In healthy families, there are no black sheep. Our goal isn't to crank out two or three kids who fit some predetermined mold—but to discover, develop, and affirm each family member's uniqueness. ❧

BILL HYBELS

Children do not exist to please us.
They are not for us at all. Rather, we exist
for them—to protect them now and to
prepare them for the future.

WALTER WANGERIN, JR.

$\mathcal{L}$avish affection on your children!
Children can't be hugged and kissed too
much by both Mom and Dad. Affection is the
medium of acceptance.

BARBARA HUGHES

We will give an account to God for our own actions—not our children's reactions. I like to remind myself, as a parent, that God holds me responsible *to*, not *for*, my children!

LEE EZELL
Pills for Parents in Pain

A new command I give you:
Love one another. As I have loved you,
so you must love one another.

JESUS, JOHN 13:34

Godliness does not come

any more naturally to us than

it does to our children.

LUANNE SHACKLEFORD
A Survivor's Guide to Home Schooling

A mother is a sage who is wise enough to know when her son has reached the stage at which he would rather die than be kissed in public. 🙢

LOUISE SHATTUCK

You can't schedule a small child the way
you schedule a committee meeting.

JOSH MCDOWELL

Encouraging and equipping is not the same

as pampering and indulging.

SUSAN HUNT
Spiritual Mothering

The Lord is righteous in all his ways and loving toward all he has made. The Lord is near to all who call on him, to all who call on him in truth. He fulfills the desires of those who fear him; he hears their cry and saves them.

PSALM 145:17-19

Parent is a synonym for motivator.
Let's keep doing it.

CHARLES SWINDOLL
The Strong Family

God knows—and you ought to know—
that all you can do is your best.

LUANNE SHACKLEFORD

*P*arents aren't here to accommodate their children, but rather to love them, lead them and teach them. 🍃

ELLEN BANKS ELWELL
The Christian Mom's Idea Book

$\mathcal{W}$hen ordinary mothers pray,

extraordinary things happen.

CHERI FULLER

Whatever you do,

work at it with all your heart,

as working for the Lord....

COLOSSIANS 3:23

It's never too late to write your children a love letter, no matter what age or sex they may be. . . . No one can resist words of unconditional love.

JUDITH HAYES

To say you're a mother and homemaker is like a dirty word today. I don't want moms to feel there's no glory in that. My grandmother showed me this is a very prestigious gig we have. Our children desperately need us. I say, grab hold and enjoy!

DENIECE WILLIAMS

Our children copy everything we do.
This is one of the most terrifying
truths of parenthood.

RAY PRITCHARD

Most children spell love T, I, M, and E. To kids, the present is all there is—and our availability communicates love. ❧

H. NORMAN WRIGHT
AND GARY J. OLIVER, PH.D.
Kids Have Feelings Too

He who dwells in the shelter of the
Most High will rest in the
shadow of the Almighty.

PSALM 91:1

God gave us children as a blessing,
not a chore. As we allow ourselves to
enjoy them, we will be blessed,
refreshed, and motivated to continue
with this challenge of parenting.

JANIS MEREDITH

Our children are the only possessions we

will be able to take with us to heaven.

RON DICIANNI
Tell Me the Story

We should deal with children in
such a way that they do not fear
their parents, but that they know
they are offending God if they do
not fear their parents.

MARTIN LUTHER

The Lord your God is with you, he is mighty to save. He will take great delight in you, he will quiet you with his love, he will rejoice over you with singing.

ZEPHANIAH 3:17

An open, accepting soul
is like a well-lit home on a
cold, dark night.

R. KENT HUGHES

A mother is a master mechanic who can

get a trouser leg out of a bicycle chain

and fix anything with cellophane

tape and a hairpin.

LOUISE SHATTUCK

God gives you the children he does so they might be used as tools in your life to help you become the woman God's created you to be. Sometimes it's the most difficult child who's used by God for his special purpose in your life. ❧

SUSAN YATES

Beauty is a fading thing at best.
But the fear of God reigning in the heart
is the beauty of the soul . . . and is,
in his sight, of great price.

MATTHEW HENRY

Our tendency to self-sufficiency

can only be overcome when

our situation is beyond

our sufficiency.

SUSAN HUNT
Spiritual Mothering

$\mathcal{I}$ prayed for this child, and the Lord has

granted me what I asked of him.

1 SAMUEL 1:27

To belittle is to be little.

ANONYMOUS

Don't stifle your silliness when you feel the need to tell a dumb joke or to grab your child and dance around the kitchen. Your kids will love it, and you'll have fun acting like a kid again.

JANIS MEREDITH

I am only one, you are only one. But because we are in a family we hold a piece of the puzzle in our own power. And what we can do, we should do. ❧

J. ALLAN PETERSON
The Strong Family

Listening to a child is more than
the absence of talking.

RON HUTCHCRAFT
5 Needs Your Child Must Have Met at Home

Every good and perfect gift is from above, coming down from the Father of the heavenly lights, who does not change like shifting shadows.

JAMES 1:17

Home is about making a place hallowed,

where people feel comfortable and

safe and can grow.

DENALYN LUCADO

Be completely humble and gentle;
be patient, bearing with one
another in love.

EPHESIANS 4:2

I t is better to be hated for telling the truth than to be loved for telling a lie.

ADRIAN ROGERS

Ten Secrets for a Successful Family

The most effective parents are those
who have the skill to get behind the
eyes of their child, seeing what he
sees, thinking what he thinks,
feeling what he feels.

JAMES DOBSON
The New Dare to Discipline

Do not judge, and you will not be judged.
Do not condemn, and you will not be
condemned. Forgive, and you
will be forgiven.

JESUS, LUKE 6:37

We have to do our very best, and
then let God do the rest.

LUANNE SHACKLEFORD
A Survivor's Guide to Home Schooling

In our home, we could ask any question without being belittled and question any answer without being condemned. But we could not say "I can't." Failure was allowed, but we were always expected to try.

GLORIA GAITHER

Without the Way, there is no going;
without the Truth, there is no knowing;
without the Life, there is no living.

THOMAS À KEMPIS
The Strong Family

Train a child in the way he should
go, and when he is old, he
will not turn from it.

I've discovered that the key to effective parenting can be summed up in one loaded sentence: Look beyond your child's deeds to his needs.

RON HUTCHCRAFT

Encouragement is one of the most
powerful gifts you can give your children.
It is a gift that nurtures competence
and confidence and optimism.

JANIS LONG HARRIS
What Good Parents Have in Common

$\mathcal{P}$ositive sibling relationships begin with

parents who model fairness.

JAY KESLER

❧

Life is a splendid gift. There is nothing small in it. For the greatest grow by God's law out of the smallest. ❧

FLORENCE NIGHTINGALE

Your bond with your kids will be
strengthened when you experience
something together.

JANIS MEREDITH

"For I know the plans I have for you,"
declares the Lord, "plans to prosper
you and not to harm you, plans
to give you hope and a future."

JEREMIAH 29:11

To be firm but fair always allows for failure. When children feel they can never fail, they're hampered and become afraid to try, risk, create, grow and learn. When parents are understanding, they can turn a failure into a good learning situation. ❧

DR. KEVIN LEMAN
Bringing Up Kids Without Tearing Them Down

It is we who must give to the children—by lovely laughter, by laughter utterly free, and by the sheer joy from which such laughter springs—the lasting memory: You are, you are, you are, my child, a marvelous work of God.

WALTER WANGERIN, JR.

Invariably, parents make two common mistakes. First, they use the same approach with all their children. Secondly, they compare them with other children. Both mistakes stem from not knowing them, from failing to see their individual bents.

CHARLES SWINDOLL

The way you make anything not boring is to use your imagination. We find that's what kids are best at. They instruct us at the level of the imagination as much or more than we do them.

MICHAEL CARD

O Lord, our Lord, how majestic is your name in all the earth! You have set your glory above the heavens. From the lips of children and infants you have ordained praise. . . .

PSALM 8:1-2A

Wise parents will talk about God
throughout the day and talk
with him in the presence
of their children.

JOHN AND CAROL DETTONI
Parents Resource Bible

If children are going to be free to enjoy their childhood and develop at their God-given pace, we must abandon the notion that they should be pushed to outshine their peers. In some cases, a well-meaning push to succeed . . . squeezes the precious gift of innocence out of them. ❧

DOUG FIELDS
Parents Resource Bible

The healthy heart of an individual as well as the heart of our civilization itself depends on good mothering. Without a deep commitment to having and raising children, our world will not survive.

GRACE KETTERMAN, M.D.
Parents Resource Bible

Heredity does not equip a child
with proper attitudes; children
learn what they are taught.

JAMES DOBSON
The New Dare to Discipline

*A commitment to marriage is
the first step to building
a strong family.*

ROLF ZETTERSTEN
Parents Resource Bible

Her children arise and call her blessed;

her husband also, and he praises her.

PROVERBS 31:28

Don't allow the mundane or the frantic
to rob you of a joyful family life.
Don't let the hope of "someday"
distract you from the
blessings of today.

KURT BRUNER
Parents Resource Bible

If you want to make sure your kids know you have ears that hear them, try this: Listen with your eyes. If you say, "I'm listening," and want your family to know you mean it, your eyes must say it too. ❧

JOHN TRENT

One good mother is worth a

hundred schoolmasters.

C. H. SPURGEON

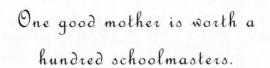

Whoever welcomes one of these little children in my name welcomes me; and whoever welcomes me does not welcome me, but the one who sent me.

JESUS, MARK 9:37

*P*arents know that children rank the words *not yet* as nearly the most awful in the English language, second only to the word *no*.

BILL HYBELS
Too Busy Not to Pray

What makes us discontented with our condition is the absurdly exaggerated idea we have of the happiness of others. 🐦

ANONYMOUS

No parent is perfect. But if you honor your children on a consistent basis, their sense of value will overshadow your mistakes.

GARY SMALLEY
Parents Resource Bible

A mother's heart has many reasons
to fear—each one an opportunity
to step out in faith.

UNKNOWN

$\mathcal{D}$o not let your hearts be troubled.

Trust in God; trust also in me.

JESUS, JOHN 14:1

The Lord bless you and keep you;

the Lord make his face shine

upon you and be gracious to you;

the Lord turn his face toward you

and give you peace.

NUMBERS 6:24-26